CW01239121

Original title:
The Solstice Calm

Copyright © 2024 Swan Charm
All rights reserved.

Author: Aron Pilviste
ISBN HARDBACK: 978-9908-1-1831-4
ISBN PAPERBACK: 978-9908-1-1832-1
ISBN EBOOK: 978-9908-1-1833-8

Unfolding Under a Blanket of Stars

Beneath the sky's vast, twinkling hue,
Laughter dances, spirits renew.
Joyful voices rise and cheer,
Celebrations fill the atmosphere.

Fireflies weave through the night,
With lanterns aglow, a beautiful sight.
Friends gather round, sharing their dreams,
As magic unfolds in shimmering beams.

The music plays, hearts feel alive,
In this festive moment, hopes thrive.
Together we bask in love's embrace,
Under the stars, we find our place.

A Journey into the Quiet

In the stillness of dawn's soft light,
Whispers of hope take flight.
Colors blend in gentle streams,
As silence hums with secret dreams.

With every step, the world slows down,
Nature wears her quiet crown.
A path of leaves, a tune so clear,
Guides us forward through warmth and cheer.

In solitude, we find our way,
The heart unveils what words can't say.
With each moment, we connect anew,
In this tranquil joy, our spirits grew.

Time Paused Between Seasons

As winter whispers to spring's caress,
Nature holds her breath in blessedness.
Blossoms ready to burst and bloom,
In this fleeting pause, we feel the room.

Sunlight kisses the frost away,
Birds sing bright, welcoming the day.
Colors clash in a vibrant fight,
In the dance of change, pure delight.

Mirth fills the air, laughter is free,
Every heartbeat sings of glee.
Between the times, we celebrate,
This joyful moment we create.

The Glow of Solitary Candles

In the dark, a flickering flame,
Each candle whispers a name.
Light spills warmth, soft and bright,
Illuminating paths in the night.

Gathered close, hearts intertwine,
In solitude, we find the divine.
With each glow, stories are told,
Of hopes and dreams, both young and old.

The gentle dance of light brings peace,
In its embrace, the world's burdens cease.
A moment shared, a spirit set free,
In this glowing warmth, we find unity.

Hushed Moments of Winter's Veil

Snowflakes drift like whispers soft,
Covering earth in a quiet loft.
Footprints fade in the shimmering white,
As joy dances in the lingering night.

Candles flicker with a warm embrace,
Families gather in a cherished space.
Laughter blends with the evening's song,
In these moments, we truly belong.

Stillness Before the Firelight

Logs crackle, casting shadows tall,
The fire whispers tales, enchanting all.
Mugs of cocoa held close in hands,
As cozy warmth around us expands.

Frost paints windows with a silvery hue,
Outside the world wears a blanket anew.
Hearts are light, and spirits soar high,
Together we bask in moments that fly.

A Breath of Winter's Embrace

In the brisk air, memories glide,
Every snowflake a joyful ride.
Children's laughter echoes through trees,
As winter's magic dances with ease.

Twinkling lights adorn every street,
The spirit of joy in each heartbeat.
Nature rests beneath frozen covers,
Yet bonds grow strong among loving brothers.

Celestial Harmony in the Quiet

Stars twinkle softly in the dark,
Each one a wish, a hopeful spark.
The moon glows bright, a guardian warm,
Guiding dreams like a protective charm.

Silent nights wrapped in a gentle embrace,
With every breath, we find our place.
In stillness, we savor the magic that rolls,
Hushed moments of winter fill our souls.

The Browning Leaves of Dusk

Golden leaves swirl in playful dance,
As twilight paints the sky with chance.
Laughter echoes through the air,
In the crisp embrace, we all share.

Candles flicker, warmth ignites,
Gathered close, we share delights.
Stories woven, hearts entwine,
In this moment, all is divine.

Whispers Between Two Worlds.

Stars awaken in the velvet night,
As shadows blend, both dark and light.
We share smiles, secrets unfold,
In whispers soft, our dreams are told.

The moon adorned in silver hue,
Guides our thoughts, both old and new.
Celebrating what we hold dear,
With every laugh, we draw near.

Whispers of the Longest Night

Underneath a blanket of deep blue,
The world slows down, a gentle view.
Fires crackle, warmth surrounds,
In the stillness, joy abounds.

With every twinkle in the sky,
A promise made, we won't say goodbye.
Wrapped in love, festivity's glow,
Together, onward, we'll always go.

Cradled in Twilight's Embrace

As day fades soft into the night,
Laughter blossoms, hearts take flight.
Candied treats and sweet delight,
We share our dreams till morning light.

In the dance of dusk, we rejoice,
Hands entwined, we find our voice.
Every moment, a treasure to keep,
Together, in joy, we softly leap.

The Language of Frost and Light

Whispers of snowflakes dance in the air,
Glittering diamonds, memories rare.
Laughter erupts in the chill of the night,
A symphony sparkling, our hearts take flight.

Candles flicker with warmth and delight,
Illuminating faces in soft, golden light.
Carols resound, filling spaces with cheer,
In the company of loved ones, the magic is here.

Breaths of Hibernation

Under the blanket of a soft, white sheen,
The world embraces a velvety dream.
Whispers of stillness weave through the pines,
Nature's secret lullaby, where joy intertwines.

Gathered around fires, tales warmly unfold,
Stories of laughter, adventures retold.
A dance of the embers, the night takes its flight,
In the glow of the hearth, hearts shine so bright.

Solstice Reflections in Still Waters

Beneath the moon's gaze, in calm waters flow,
Reflections of joy in the evening's soft glow.
Stars in their splendor twinkle above,
Nature's embrace, a promise of love.

The air filled with scents of pine and of spice,
Warmth from within, oh, it feels so nice.
Gathering moments, beneath the starlight,
The solstice magic, pure and bright.

The Calm of Nature's Retreat

In the stillness of woods, a secret we find,
Where whispers of nature quiet the mind.
Frost on the branches, a glistening sight,
The world slows down, bathed in soft light.

The crunch of dry leaves underfoot brings a smile,
A moment of peace that lingers a while.
In harmony's embrace, all worries rescind,
As the spirit of joy and serenity blend.

The Stillness of Reflective Waters

In the twilight glow, reflections dance,
Ripples shimmer, inviting a glance.
Laughter echoes across the bay,
As twilight whispers, bidding day sway.

Candles flicker, soft in the breeze,
Frogs croon joy by the swaying trees.
The moon joins the fun, a luminous friend,
While night wraps the world in a gentle blend.

Balloons afloat, colors in flight,
Children's laughter, pure delight.
The water mirrors each joyful shout,
As hearts brim over, fears cast out.

Night unveils its silken attire,
Festive glows ignite the fire.
Each moment savored, etched in time,
In stillness, we flourish, joyfully climb.

A Canvas of Stars and Silence

Stars twinkle bright in the velvet sky,
Painting dreams from wings that fly.
The whispers of night weave a sweet song,
As waves of quiet carry us along.

Each constellation tells tales untold,
Of brave little hearts and spirits bold.
Beneath this vast celestial dome,
We gather together, in awe, we roam.

Lanterns sway, a soft golden glow,
Guiding our feet where the mysteries flow.
With every step, the magic unfolds,
In the canvas of night, adventure beholds.

Laughter unites us, warm and bright,
In the stillness, hearts take flight.
Together we dance under stars' embrace,
In this cosmic festival, we find our place.

Caressed by the Winter's Breath

Snowflakes tumble, soft as a kiss,
Blanketing earth in a serene bliss.
Families gather, warmth in the air,
With stories and laughter, love is shared.

Fires crackle, embers glow,
Peaceful moments, a gentle flow.
The world wrapped in white, a fairy tale,
As we sip hot cocoa, delights unveil.

Children play, angels in snow,
Building memories, spirits aglow.
Each frosty breath whispers sweet cheer,
As winter's magic draws us near.

In the still night, stars blaze bright,
Guiding our hearts with soft, glowing light.
Together we cherish, together we stand,
Caressed by winter, hand in hand.

Remnants of Light in the Shadows

As dusk unfurls its velvet cover,
Faint twinkles dance, like a lover.
Whispers of warmth in the night air,
Illuminate dreams, dissolve each care.

Shadows play tricks, yet hearts ignite,
In the flickering glow, spirits take flight.
Each breeze carries laughter, sweet as wine,
In this moment, all hearts align.

Lanterns aglow in the evening fall,
Stories of friendship, shared by all.
Echoes of joy in the night sky soar,
Remnants of light, there's always more.

We raise our cups to the stars above,
In unity, we celebrate love.
Among shadows and light, we laugh and sing,
In this festival, life's wonders we bring.

The Essence of Silent Transformation

In the hush of dawn's bright gleam,
Colors dance in the sun's warm beam.
Whispers of change float through the air,
Nature dons her festive glare.

With each flutter of leaf and bloom,
Joy spills forth, dispelling gloom.
Butterflies twirl in a vibrant trance,
As life awakes in a fleeting chance.

Fields adorned in golden hues,
Remind the heart of joyful news.
Laughter echoes in the gentle breeze,
Harmony sways among the trees.

Silent transformations, spirit bright,
Invite us all to share the light.
In every moment, new dreams arise,
Underneath the vast, embracing sky.

Night's Embrace Holding the World

Stars peek through a velvet veil,
As night weaves its enchanting tale.
Moonlight dances on silver streams,
Carrying whispers of radiant dreams.

The air hums with magic's call,
Inviting souls to joyously sprawl.
Each heartbeat syncs with the night,
As shadows twirl in ethereal light.

Bonfires crackle, stories unfold,
Laughter shared, memories bold.
Embers glow in a festive glee,
Holding the world in serenity.

With each passing hour, we unite,
In the warmth of the shared delight.
Night's embrace, a cherished space,
Revealing love's gentle grace.

Reflections on Solitude's Canvas

In quiet corners, thoughts arise,
Painted dreams in tranquil skies.
Brushes soft in solitude's sway,
Crafting colors that light the way.

Quiet moments, softly embraced,
Canvas of life, beautifully traced.
Each stroke whispers, a tale to tell,
In solitude's charm, we find ourselves.

Echoes of laughter fill the air,
Even in stillness, joy is there.
The heartbeats pulse, a silent tune,
Inviting echoes beneath the moon.

With every hue, reflections gleam,
Invoking visions, a vibrant dream.
In solitude's arms, we learn to be,
In the essence of life, wild and free.

The Peaceful Interlude of the Year

In the hush of twilight glow,
Families gather, warmth in tow.
Laughter dances in the air,
Joyful moments, free from care.

Candles flicker, hearts ignite,
Wishes carried on the night.
Songs of love, a sweet refrain,
Binding souls like gentle chain.

A Dance of Light and Dark

Stars awaken, skies unfolding,
Whispers of the night enfolding.
Moonlight spills like silver wine,
In this dance, our spirits shine.

Shadows flicker, laughter swirls,
In our hearts, the magic twirls.
Together we share this embrace,
A festive night, a timeless space.

Moments Suspended in Stillness

Quiet pauses, breaths we take,
In the stillness, hearts awake.
Time slows down, the world ignites,
Every second, pure delight.

Through the window, snowflakes glide,
Soft and gentle, like love's tide.
Gathered close, we share bright dreams,
In this moment, joy redeems.

Soft Hues of Winter's Breath

Colors merge in twilight's grace,
Winter's magic fills the space.
Frosty breath, a canvas white,
Healing hearts in soft twilight.

Joyful cheers and playful cheer,
Friends and family drawing near.
In these hues, our laughter flows,
Winter's warmth, our love bestows.

The Harmony of Silent Woods

In the woods where whispers dwell,
A tapestry of stories to tell.
Leaves are dancing, skies are bright,
Nature's chorus, pure delight.

Joyful creatures play and sing,
Every heart alive, they bring.
Underneath the starlit show,
Magic blooms wherever we go.

Laughter echoes through the trees,
Carried softly by the breeze.
Each moment glows, a timeless gift,
In harmony, our spirits lift.

Gatherings of Light in the Cold

As the snowflakes gently fall,
Gatherings await, smiles for all.
Lanterns flicker, warmth in air,
Every heart rejoices there.

Chilled cheeks, laughter so bright,
Together we share our light.
Around the fire, tales unfold,
In every moment, love we hold.

Cocoa sipped, hands entwined,
In this season, joy we find.
Shadows dance, spirits rise,
In gatherings of light, we prize.

A Melody for Resting Dreams

In twilight's glow, the world does rest,
A lullaby for every quest.
Stars above in soft embrace,
Whispering dreams, our special place.

Moonlight weaves through silent trees,
Carrying thoughts on gentle breeze.
Close your eyes, let troubles drift,
In this moment, find your gift.

Melodies of peace align,
In the night, our hearts entwine.
With every breath, sweet solace stirs,
A tranquil world, where joy occurs.

Frozen Symphony of the Night

In the night where snowflakes gleam,
A frozen world holds a dream.
Nature's choir sings so sweet,
Echoing the winter's beat.

Starlit skies above our heads,
A symphony of silent threads.
Each flake dances, stars ignite,
Creating magic, pure delight.

With every breath, the air is still,
The night embraces, whispers thrill.
In frozen beauty, hearts ignite,
A symphony of pure delight.

Awakened Spirits in the Dark

Under the moon, the shadows sway,
Laughter dances in playful sway.
Colors burst in a vibrant spark,
Awakened spirits in the dark.

Fireflies twinkle, lights aglow,
Joyful echoes in the winds that blow.
Hearts connected in this sacred arc,
Awakened spirits in the dark.

Tunes of mirth wrap round the night,
Every soul glimmers with delight.
In the hush, life's sweet remark,
Awakened spirits in the dark.

Cheers resound, the night's embrace,
Filling every cherished space.
Together bound, igniting a spark,
Awakened spirits in the dark.

Weightless Whispers of Winter

Snowflakes drift on a gentle breeze,
Softly falling from silent trees.
Whispers float through the chilly air,
Weightless whispers, winter's prayer.

Twinkling lights adorn each street,
Joyful laughter, hearts skip a beat.
Kisses shared by fireside flare,
Weightless whispers, winter's prayer.

Children's laughter in the white,
Frolic and play in pure delight.
Every moment, a memory rare,
Weightless whispers, winter's prayer.

As the world wears a quilt of snow,
Dreams take flight, as spirits glow.
In this magic, we find our care,
Weightless whispers, winter's prayer.

Kindred Spirits in Still Nights

Under the stars, our laughter swirls,
Nighttime magic as the universe unfurls.
Kindred souls share tales so bright,
In still nights, a warm delight.

Candles flicker, shadows play,
Echoes of joy that gently stay.
Voices blend in perfect harmony,
In still nights, we feel so free.

Footprints in the soft, cool sand,
Every heartbeat, a gentle hand.
Moments woven in soft twilight,
In still nights, love takes flight.

Embraced by whispers of the dark,
Together we dance, we leave our mark.
Kindred spirits in purest sight,
In still nights, our hearts unite.

Winter's Breath on My Windowpane

The world outside is a frosty canvas,
Breath of winter, a chill that amass.
I watch the frost with a smile so plain,
Winter's breath on my windowpane.

The glow of lanterns, warm and bright,
Welcoming joy on this crisp night.
Hot cocoa sipped, a sweet refrain,
Winter's breath on my windowpane.

Snowflakes twirl in a graceful dance,
Each one unique, a perfect chance.
Memories linger, like soft champagne,
Winter's breath on my windowpane.

Laughter lingers, as stories weave,
In the glow of love, we believe.
In this season, all hearts remain,
Winter's breath on my windowpane.

Whispers of the Longest Night

Underneath twinkling stars so bright,
Laughter dances through the night.
Warm fires crackle, stories unfold,
In every heart, joy takes hold.

Soft carols drift on the breeze,
Frosty whispers in the trees.
Families gather, spirits high,
Wishing on the moonlit sky.

Candles flicker, shadows play,
Magic flows through holiday.
A tapestry of love we weave,
In this moment, we believe.

As the clock chimes midnight's song,
Hope and laughter all night long.
In our hearts, the warmth ignites,
Whispers linger of this night.

Embrace of the Frosted Dawn

Soft light breaks the silent dawn,
Frosted glimmers on the lawn.
Joyful cheers fill the air,
In each heart, love's warmth to share.

Children's laughter, bright and clear,
Echoing joy as they draw near.
Winter's chill can't dampen cheer,
For the season draws us near.

Brightly wrapped gifts and playful glee,
In every smile, a memory.
Gentle hugs, a cozy glow,
In this moment, love will flow.

As sunlight waltzes on the snow,
Together in the warmth we grow.
In sweet embrace, we'll find our way,
Trusting in this perfect day.

Equinox Echoes

Golden leaves beneath our feet,
Festive spirits, hearts will meet.
Candles glow as shadows fade,
Unity in moments made.

Bonfires blaze with stories told,
Gathered close, we brave the cold.
Warmth of laughter in the night,
Guiding stars, our hearts take flight.

Harvest joy in every hand,
Together we shall firmly stand.
Songs of old and tales anew,
In the echoes, friendships grew.

As daylight dances with the night,
We celebrate in pure delight.
Equinox whispers secrets sweet,
In this gathering, life's complete.

Shadows in Serene Silence

In the hush of quiet nights,
Glistening snow, the world ignites.
Unity in silence blooms,
Underneath the starlit rooms.

Footsteps soft on frosty ground,
Joyful hearts are tightly bound.
Warm embraces, candle's gleam,
In this stillness, we can dream.

Whispers fade, yet laughter stays,
In the glow of winter's haze.
Let the soft breeze take its flight,
As we bask in sheer delight.

With every hug and shared smile bright,
Shadows lift in the soft light.
Together, we'll face this night,
In serene bliss, all feels right.

Secrets of the Charmed Winter

Whispers of snowflakes dance and glide,
Snowmen smile with joy and pride.
Under twinkling lights so bright,
Secrets unfold in winter's night.

Children laugh and play outside,
Sleds and laughter, hearts open wide.
In warm cabins, stories are spun,
A tapestry of joy, all in one.

Cups of cocoa steaming high,
With marshmallows floating, oh my!
The crisp air sings a merry tune,
Under the gaze of the glowing moon.

Fires crackle, embers bright,
Keeping dreams alive tonight.
The charms of winter, we hold dear,
In every moment, love draws near.

Radiance in the Quiet of Night

Stars sprinkle silver in the dark,
Moonlight leaves its shimmering mark.
In the stillness, joy abounds,
Magic whispers in silent sounds.

Fires burn with a soft glow,
Crickets chirp their gentle show.
Families gather, hearts align,
Creating memories, sweet and divine.

Cool breezes carry laughter high,
As dreams take flight, the night is nigh.
With every smile, the world feels right,
Radiance shines in the calm of night.

The warmth of love, a glowing flame,
In this quiet, nothing's the same.
As shadows dance, our spirits lift,
In unity, we find our gift.

The Art of Stillness

In the hush of twilight's glow,
Nature pauses, soft and slow.
Gentle breezes brush the trees,
The world whispers with such ease.

Stillness holds a sacred space,
Where moments quiet, find their grace.
With every breath, a soft release,
In the art of stillness, we find peace.

Clouds drift lazily in the sky,
Birds sing gently as they fly.
Here in silence, hearts ignite,
Finding beauty in the night.

With open minds and softened hearts,
We learn where stillness truly starts.
In each heartbeat, we discover,
The quiet art that brings us closer.

Frosty Breath of the Ancients

In the chill, the whispers rise,
Frosty breath beneath wide skies.
Ancient tales of winter's breath,
Hold the wisdom of life and death.

Branches glisten, crystal clear,
Nature's wonders drawing near.
In the moonlight, shadows play,
Echoes of the past lead the way.

The frozen ground, a canvas bright,
Holds the stories of the night.
Footprints fade but memories stay,
In frost and beauty, come what may.

Gather round the fire's glow,
As tales of old begin to flow.
In the frosty air, take delight,
The ancients dance in the starry light.

Serenity Wrapped in White

Snowflakes dance in gentle air,
Blanketing earth with tender care.
Children laugh and frolic wide,
In this wonder, hearts abide.

Twinkling lights adorn the night,
Warmth and joy, a pure delight.
Friends gather 'round the hearth's glow,
Sharing stories, soft and slow.

Mugs of cocoa, sweet and warm,
Embracing love, a cozy charm.
The world transformed, in purest white,
Serenity wrapped in festive light.

A Stillness like No Other

The world is hushed, as shadows play,
Soft whispers greet the end of day.
Stars awaken in the deep,
A stillness wraps the night in sleep.

Candles flicker, casting glow,
Laughter echoes, soft and low.
Memories made, laughter shared,
In this moment, hearts are bared.

Outside the world wears winter's grace,
Each breath a cloud, a gentle lace.
In quiet joy, we find our peace,
A stillness that will never cease.

Reflections on the Frosted Glass

Windows glisten with icy art,
Nature paints with a silent heart.
Gleaming paths of crystal bright,
Reflecting dreams in sacred light.

Children press their hands to see,
Magic formed in winter's spree.
Outside, a world of purest dreams,
Inside, warmth and laughter gleams.

Whispers of joy fill the air,
Every moment, a treasure rare.
Reflections dance on frosted glass,
In this magic, time will pass.

Beneath the Silent Boughs

Underneath the boughs so still,
Snowflakes gather, hearts to fill.
Nature rests in deep embrace,
Finding joy in winter's grace.

Fires crackle, stories flow,
Families share the warmth they know.
Beneath the stars, dreams unfurl,
A timeless bond within this swirl.

Seasons shift, yet here we stand,
Hand in hand, a promised land.
Beneath the silent boughs we find,
A festive peace that warms the mind.

Breath of Winter's Tranquil Heart

Snowflakes twirl in joyful dance,
Whispers of peace in the winter's glance.
Fires crackle with cheerful light,
Bringing warmth on this frosty night.

Families gather, laughter spills,
In cozy corners, the heart surely thrills.
In every hug, a story shared,
A tapestry of love, carefully paired.

Outside, the world is a glittering dream,
Each branch adorned with nature's gleam.
With every breath, the magic grows,
Winter's embrace, a soft repose.

As stars emerge in the velvet sky,
Hope takes flight, like birds on high.
In this moment, all feels right,
Heartbeats echo against the night.

The Solace in Starry Silence

Under the canvas of midnight's veil,
Whispers of wonders, secrets unveil.
Starlit skies, like diamonds strewn,
Guide our hearts to a gentle tune.

Each flicker tells tales of old,
Of dreams and wishes, bright and bold.
The moon grins down with soft embrace,
Wrapping night in a tranquil grace.

Crickets sing in a chorus of night,
Nature's lullaby, pure delight.
In tranquil corners, the stillness reigns,
Filling our souls, healing the pains.

As we bask in this serene glow,
Together, we drift, destined to flow.
Holding hands under cosmic sights,
Finding solace in starry nights.

Midnight's Quiet Reverie

In the hush of the midnight hour,
Dreams awaken, bloom like flower.
Shadows dance in soft moonlight,
Whispering secrets deep in the night.

The world is hushed, a canvas bare,
Each heartbeat echoes with tender care.
Thoughts take flight on night's cool breeze,
Unraveling worries, bringing ease.

Stars twinkle softly, a soft serenade,
Filling the heart where echoes fade.
In this stillness, joy's embraced,
Time slows down, no moment's waste.

Midnight crafts a wondrous spell,
In silence, we weave our story well.
Together, we bask in dreams so bright,
In the embrace of this lovely night.

When Time Pauses at Dusk

As daylight fades to a soft embrace,
Colors blend with tender grace.
The sun bows low, a golden sphere,
Painting the sky, our hearts draw near.

Cool breezes stir, whispers of cheer,
In this moment, there's nothing to fear.
Nature sighs, a symphony sweet,
With every heartbeat, the world feels complete.

Children laugh and shadows play,
Chasing dreams at the close of day.
Fireflies flicker in twilight's glow,
Magic unfolds, as time runs slow.

Gathered close as dusk descends,
Every heart knows, this feeling transcends.
In the soft twilight, love does bloom,
A kind of joy that brightens the gloom.

Echoes of Serenity

Banners flying in the breeze,
Laughter dances through the trees.
Colors bright, a joyful sight,
Hearts unite in pure delight.

Candles glow with warmth and cheer,
Whispers of good wishes near.
Voices rise in sweet refrain,
Echoes join like gentle rain.

Joyful faces, smiles abound,
Magic lingers all around.
In this moment, time stands still,
Wishes granted, dreams fulfill.

As the stars twinkle above,
We celebrate the gift of love.
In the night, our spirits soar,
Echoes of joy forevermore.

Dawning Hopes in the Frost

Morning breaks with golden light,
Frosty air feels pure and bright.
Crystals shimmer on the ground,
New beginnings all around.

Gathered friends in warmth and cheer,
Laughter ringing, loud and clear.
Hope ignites in every heart,
From this day, we won't depart.

Songs of joy in winter's chill,
Grateful hearts with strength and will.
Together hand in hand we stand,
Building dreams, a future planned.

As the sunlight starts to glow,
Frolic through the shining snow.
Dawning hopes, our dreams take flight,
Embracing all the sheer delight.

Tidings of Stillness

Softly falls the winter snow,
Whispers dance where cool winds blow.
Silent nights with stars so bright,
Spirits lift in pure delight.

Gather close, the warmth we share,
Tidings wrap us, love laid bare.
In this stillness, hearts combine,
Moments cherished, pure divine.

Crisp and clear, the air is sweet,
Joyful rhythms in our feet.
While the world slows down its pace,
In this calm, we find our place.

With the moon as our soft guide,
Together, we shall find our stride.
Tidings of stillness linger near,
In the quiet, we hold dear.

Lanterns of Winter's Dream

Lanterns glowing, softly bright,
Casting warmth on winter's night.
Chilly air wrapped all around,
Yet in joy, our hearts are found.

Stories shared by flick'ring flame,
Each one cherished, none the same.
Laughter echoes through the dark,
In our souls, we light a spark.

As the frosty winds may sigh,
Hopeful dreams begin to fly.
With each lantern, tales unfold,
Moments precious, hearts of gold.

In this season, joy can bloom,
Find your light, break through the gloom.
Lanterns guide us ever on,
In winter's dream, we greet the dawn.

Stars Gather to Whisper Secrets

In the velvet sky, they gleam,
A dance of lights, a twinkling dream.
With laughter soft, they share their tales,
Wisdom borne on moonlit trails.

Each star a friend, shining bright,
Glistening hope in the deepening night.
They weave together, a tapestry fine,
In cosmic rhythms, their secrets align.

Beneath this canopy, hearts take flight,
Warmed by the glow of celestial light.
Joy and wonder fill the air,
An endless dance, a moment rare.

As dreams are whispered across the space,
In every glance, a trace of grace.
United in joy, we gaze in awe,
While stars gather close, in silence draw.

Timeless Slumber of the Earth

In twilight's embrace, the world is still,
Nature's heart beats, soft and chill.
The trees sway gently, in peaceful dreams,
Wrapped in moonlight's tender beams.

Fields of flowers close their eyes,
Beneath a blanket of starry skies.
Whispers of night, a lullaby sweet,
Crickets chirp in rhythmic beat.

Each creature rests, in shadows cast,
While time floats gently, moments passed.
The world transforms in quiet grace,
A festive night, a warm embrace.

In slumber deep, the Earth renews,
Cradling dreams, casting hues.
Beneath this magic, peace, and cheer,
The timeless slumber holds us near.

An Echo of Nature's Whispering Calm

In the forest deep, a secret lies,
A symphony played beneath the skies.
Leaves rustle gently, in soft refrain,
Nature's echo calls through the grain.

The brook babbles tunes, sweet and bright,
Carried by winds in the fading light.
Each breath a gift, the air so clear,
Serenading hearts, drawing us near.

Mountains stand tall, draped in gold,
Guardians of stories yet untold.
With every whisper, the earth's embrace,
In calm reflection, it finds its place.

As shadows dance and daylight wanes,
A festive spirit in every vein.
In the quiet magic, we find our balm,
An echo of Nature's whispering calm.

Shadows Drawn in a Golden Glow

As suns descend and colors bloom,
Shadows stretch in their evening room.
The air is rich with laughter's sound,
In golden glow, our joys abound.

Footsteps tread on paths of light,
Each moment shared, a pure delight.
With friends beside, we dance and sing,
To the festive warmth that autumn brings.

Candles flicker in gentle glee,
Casting stories on every tree.
While fireflies twirl, a magical show,
In shadows drawn, the world will glow.

Together we weave the night's soft grace,
Painting memories, time cannot erase.
In this golden hour, hearts ignite,
Shadows drawn, under stars so bright.

Dawn's First Caress Through Frost

A gentle light unfolds the day,
As winter's chill begins to sway.
With glistening crystals on each blade,
Nature's beauty, serenely laid.

The sun peeks through, a soft embrace,
Whispers of warmth in the frosty space.
Birdsong dances in the crisp air,
A joyful start, a moment rare.

The world awakes with colors bright,
Frosty edges kissed by light.
Each breath taken, a gift anew,
In this wonderland painted blue.

Together we gather, hearts aligned,
In the magic that nature designed.
Celebrating life, as spirits soar,
Dawn's first caress, forevermore.

Tranquil Nights and Starry Sights

Beneath the velvet sky we lay,
Counting stars that gently play.
A gentle breeze whispers the night,
In tranquil peace, our hearts take flight.

Moonbeams scatter, soft and bright,
Filling our dreams with pure delight.
Nature's lullaby, a sweet refrain,
In the stillness, we feel no pain.

Crickets sing a melody fair,
As we breathe in the cool night air.
The world, a canvas of twinkling lights,
Each star aglow, our spirits ignite.

Hand in hand, beneath the sky,
In the stillness, our worries fly.
Together we dance, hearts in tune,
Amidst the magic of the moon.

Frosted Whispers in Slow Motion

The world slows down, a quiet scene,
Frosted whispers, calm and serene.
Each flake a story, softly spun,
In this moment, we're all as one.

Branches wear their coats of white,
Glistening softly, pure delight.
As snowflakes fall like dreams from above,
A reminder of peace, a token of love.

We stroll through trails, hand in hand,
Tracing moments in the winter land.
Laughter echoes on the crisp breeze,
In frosted whispers, our hearts find ease.

A tapestry woven of joy and cheer,
As we celebrate this time of year.
With every breath, magic fills the air,
In this frosted realm, we find our care.

Glistening Dreams beneath Sleeping Pines

In the hush of night, the world sleeps tight,
Beneath the pines, where dreams take flight.
Glistening snowflakes twinkle and glimmer,
As shadows fade and starlight shimmers.

A blanket of white wraps all around,
Peace and joy in silence found.
The moon casts its glow on winter's throne,
In this quietude, we're never alone.

As the gentle winds sing lullabies,
Underneath this vast, open sky.
Hopes and wishes take to the air,
In glistening dreams, we shed our care.

Together we whisper soft and low,
Beneath the trees where peace will flow.
In this enchanted, wintery shrine,
We find our dreams in the sleeping pines.

Beneath the Veil of Changing Seasons

Leaves dance down from ancient trees,
Color bursts in joyous ease.
Golden hues and crisp, cool air,
Nature's art beyond compare.

Harvest moons light up the night,
Shining bright, a splendid sight.
Friends and laughter fill the space,
In this warm, embrace of grace.

Pumpkin spice and cider warm,
Celebrations start to swarm.
Beneath the veil, we gather round,
In love and joy, we are bound.

A Lullaby for the Frozen Earth

Whispers soft in winter's night,
Stars above, a twinkling light.
Snowflakes drift like dreams untold,
Wrapping all in silken fold.

Crisp air carries warmth inside,
Where flickering fires abide.
Footsteps crunch on frosty ground,
In this hush, pure peace is found.

Lullabies the moonlight sings,
Blanketing with gentle wings.
Nature rests in quiet grace,
In this stillness, hearts embrace.

Harmonies of the Dimming Light

Colors fade as day gives way,
Sunset whispers, soft and gray.
Crickets chirp a serenade,
Night's sweet call, no need to fade.

Lanterns glow, a warm embrace,
Gathered friends in cozy space.
Laughter mingles with the sound,
In these moments, love is found.

Underneath the evening sky,
Dreams take flight, the stars will spy.
Harmony in twilight's glow,
A timeless dance, a gentle flow.

Resting in Nature's Gentle Arms

Softly bends the willow tree,
Nature cradles you and me.
Gentle breezes guide our dreams,
In this place, our spirit beams.

Flowers sway in vibrant hues,
Painting fields with morning dew.
Sunlight kisses every leaf,
In this joy, we find belief.

Cascading streams hum their song,
Inviting all to sing along.
Resting here, we bloom anew,
In life's arms, forever true.

Glimmers of Gold as Days Shorten

As autumn leaves begin to sway,
The golden light fades into gray.
We gather close, our hearts entwined,
In warmth of laughter, joy defined.

Pumpkin spice and candles glow,
The chill in air begins to grow.
Around the fire, stories shared,
In this moment, love declared.

Twinkling lights adorn the trees,
With every smile, the world agrees.
In the twilight, dreams ignite,
With glimmers of gold, our spirits alight.

As days grow short, we hold on tight,
To memories cherished, pure delight.
In every hug, in every cheer,
We celebrate the ones held dear.

Midnight's Embrace

Beneath the stars, we whisper low,
As midnight's magic starts to flow.
With every heartbeat, shadows dance,
In twilight's warmth, we take a chance.

The night's alive with laughter's song,
In the embrace, we all belong.
We twirl and spin, our spirits free,
In midnight's arms, just you and me.

Lanterns flicker, soft and bright,
Illuminating dreams in flight.
Each moment precious, memories made,
In the midnight's glow, our fears will fade.

As silence falls, the world awakes,
In festive bliss, our hearts it shapes.
We count these beats, a joyful trace,
Together, lost in midnight's embrace.

Radiance in the Depths of Dark

When shadows gather, we won't fear,
For in the dark, our light is clear.
With laughter ringing, spirits rise,
An evening bright beneath the skies.

Candles flicker, faces glow,
In every heart, a warm tableau.
We share our hopes, our joyful spark,
Creating radiance in the dark.

With every toast, with every cheer,
We wrap our dreams in love sincere.
In festive moments, bonds we weave,
Together, stronger, we believe.

As stars above begin to glow,
With every hug, our spirits flow.
In depths of dark, we find our way,
In radiant joy, we choose to stay.

The Dance of Light and Shadow

In twilight's cloak, the world transforms,
As light and shadow take their forms.
We waltz through memories, hand in hand,
In every heartbeat, love we stand.

The playful spark of candlelight,
Cuts through the dark, ignites the night.
With laughter ringing, joy's embrace,
We gather close in this sacred space.

In laughter's echo, shadows play,
As night unfolds, we drift away.
Our voices rise, a merry sound,
In the dance of dusk, our hearts are found.

As stars awaken, dreams unfold,
In every story, magic told.
Together here, we find our flow,
In the dance of light and shadow.

Moonlit Whispers

Beneath the stars, the night does gleam,
Whispers of joy, like a sweet dream.
Laughter dances in the cool air,
As friends gather round, hearts laid bare.

Glowing lanterns grace the trees,
A symphony of warmth and ease.
Moonlight waltzes on the stream,
Casting shadows, a gentle beam.

Joyous songs fill the night sky,
With every note, spirits fly.
Hands held tight, love's embrace,
In this moment, we find our place.

As dawn approaches, we shall stay,
Wrapped in memories, come what may.
Moonlit whispers, soft and light,
Festivity glows in the night.

Embracing the Chilling Air

Crisp and bright, the morning breaks,
A frosty breath, the silence wakes.
Coats wrapped tight, boots laced with care,
The world transformed, embracing the air.

Snowflakes twirl in a dazzling dance,
Children laugh, a glee-filled trance.
Sleds and snowmen, joy on display,
In the chill, we find our play.

Warm fires crackle, stories unfold,
Cocoa in hand, hearts unfold.
Laughter echoes, a festive song,
In the chilling air, we belong.

As daylight wanes, the stars appear,
Magic lingers, full of cheer.
Together we stand, a warm parade,
In the embrace of joy, unafraid.

Harmony Beneath the Blankets of Snow

Gentle layers, white and pure,
Nature's quilt, a soft allure.
Footsteps muffled, whispers bright,
Beneath the snow, hearts take flight.

Twinkling lights on trees aglow,
A festive spirit, a warm flow.
Hot cider sipped, cheeks aglow,
In this stillness, love does grow.

Laughter shared by the fireside,
Embracing warmth with hearts open wide.
Together we weave this night's grace,
In harmony's hands, we find our place.

As the world sleeps in a silent song,
We gather close, where we belong.
Beneath the blankets, stories unfold,
In this season, a joy to hold.

Unraveling Time in Quietude

In the hush of twilight's call,
Moments linger, gentle and small.
Time unwinds, a soft embrace,
Quietude dwells in this sacred space.

Candles flicker, shadows play,
Whispers echo of yesterday.
Hand in hand, we journey through,
Each heartbeat pure, the skies so blue.

With every laugh, a memory spun,
Underneath the winter sun.
Stories shared, old and new,
Within this warmth, our dreams construe.

As the night deepens, stars ignite,
In this stillness, hearts take flight.
Unraveling time, a gift we find,
In quietude, our souls entwined.

Crystal Stars and the Moonlit Path

Beneath the sky of twinkling light,
Crystal stars dance, oh so bright.
Whispers of joy fill the air,
As laughter rings without a care.

The moonlit path shimmers and glows,
Guiding feet where magic flows.
In each step, a spark ignites,
With every heart, the world unites.

The night sings soft, a gentle tune,
Celebrating life beneath the moon.
Crisp autumn leaves swirl in glee,
As dreams take flight, wild and free.

With every glance, wonder appears,
A festive spirit that calms our fears.
Together we stand, hand in hand,
In this moment, forever we'll stand.

Beneath the Canopy of Quietude

Beneath the canopy, a soft breeze flows,
Where nature whispers in dulcet prose.
The rustle of leaves, a sweet refrain,
In harmony we gather, free from pain.

Bright ribbons flutter, colors so bold,
Stories of joy and laughter retold.
Amongst the branches, stars peek through,
As we share moments, old yet new.

A table adorned with delights to share,
Laughter erupts, filling the air.
Toasting to dreams and hopes that light,
In this embrace, everything feels right.

Time slows down in the gentle night,
As we dance under the moon's soft light.
Together we bask in friendship's grace,
In this tranquil, festive, sacred space.

Embracing the Lengthening Shadows

As daylight fades, shadows extend,
We gather around, with hearts to mend.
Embracing moments, both bright and warm,
In unity, we weather the storm.

Candles flicker soft, a playful glow,
Casting warmth on faces aglow.
With stories shared, and joy in our eyes,
We celebrate life beneath the skies.

The laughter erupts, it carries afar,
In the night's embrace, we shine like a star.
With every cheer and joyful sound,
We weave a tapestry, love profound.

Together we stand as shadows grow,
In this festive spirit, we let love flow.
Hand in hand, we dance through the night,
In the lengthening shadows, hearts feel light.

Fragments of Time in the Stillness

In the stillness of quiet nights,
Fragments of time glow with delights.
Softly we gather, with stories to tell,
In laughter and warmth, we weave our spell.

The air is alive with sweet musings,
Joyful connections, no gripping fusions.
Each smile we share, a treasure released,
In the magic of now, we find our feast.

With games and music, the heartlight sings,
Celebrating simple and beautiful things.
In every glance, a moment is caught,
In fragments of joy, our souls are sought.

As stars twinkle gently in the expanse,
Each heartbeat rejoices, a vibrant dance.
In this stillness, our spirits thrive,
In the fragments of time, we come alive.

Stillness Beneath a Gilded Sky

Beneath the sun's embrace we cheer,
Children laugh, their joy sincere,
Colors dance in warm delight,
As day surrenders to the night.

Candles flicker, wishes shared,
Laughter weaves through hearts that dared,
The air is sweet with hope's soft tune,
As stars awaken, bright as noon.

Each moment sparkles, time stands still,
In this embrace, we find our thrill,
Hands held tight, we join the song,
In unity, we all belong.

Together we chase the fleeting light,
In stillness, magic takes its flight,
Beneath the gilded sky we play,
In this festive life, we find our way.

Echoes of Daylight's Farewell

Golden rays with gentle grace,
Whisper softly, night's embrace,
As shadows stretch and daylight fades,
We gather 'round in twilight glades.

Laughter rings like silver bells,
Stories shared, our hearts compel,
Echoes of joy, they fill the air,
In this moment, love lays bare.

The sky ignites in hues of red,
We dance as sunlight bows its head,
A tapestry of stars we weave,
In festal dreams, we dare believe.

Tonight we celebrate the glow,
In twilight's serenade, we flow,
With hearts united, spirits bright,
Echoes linger, the joy of night.

Serenity in Shadows' Hold

In twilight's hush, a calm descends,
Where shadows play, and laughter blends,
The world slows down, a gentle sigh,
As stars peak out in the inked sky.

We gather close, in quiet cheer,
In this stillness, magic's near,
Pumpkin spice and whispers soar,
In shadows' hold, we ask for more.

Each smile a lantern, warm and bright,
Illuminating the velvet night,
With every word, a tale we weave,
In these moments, we believe.

Together we craft this peaceful space,
With every heartbeat, time slows its race,
In serenity, our worries fade,
In festive whispers, memories made.

Frost-Kissed Dreams and Silent Stars

In chilly air, a festive glow,
Frost-kissed dreams begin to flow,
Silent stars, they twinkle proud,
Embracing joy in a whispering crowd.

Mugs of cocoa, warm and sweet,
In winter's hold, our hearts compete,
With laughter loud and spirits high,
Underneath the sapphire sky.

Snowflakes dance in the moonlight's grace,
Each flake a wish, a fleeting trace,
We gather round the fire's light,
Our hearts entwined, as day meets night.

With frost-kissed dreams, we raise a cheer,
For moments shared, we hold so dear,
In this festive night, we find our peace,
In silent stars, our joys increase.

Solitude's Warm Embers

In the corner, a fire aglow,
Whispers of warmth in the night flow.
Friends gather close, laughter and cheer,
Memories linger, each moment dear.

Crisp air dances with joy on its wings,
Stars above chime with bright diamond rings.
Songs of the season fill the air,
In solitude's embrace, love we share.

Flickering flames cast shadows so light,
Glowing hearts paint the world with delight.
Together we find our solace here,
Solitude's warmth, forever near.

As the embers fade, we'll hold on tight,
To the warmth of this blissful night.
Festive spirits in every heart,
Embracing together, never apart.

Radiant Solitude in the Chill

Beneath the moon's soft silver glow,
Snowflakes twirl in the gentle flow.
A quiet peace blankets the night,
Solitude shimmers, a sparkling sight.

Whispers of trees sway with the breeze,
Echoing laughter, a sweet tease.
In radiant calm, we find our place,
Chasing the chill with each warm embrace.

Glowing lanterns light up the dark,
Starlit paths where we leave our mark.
In this frosty realm, we share delight,
A bond so strong, it feels just right.

Memories twinkle like stars up high,
Each moment treasured as time goes by.
Radiant solitude, a festive thrill,
In the heart of winter, we find our will.

Moonlit Thoughts of Serenity

Underneath the vast sky so clear,
Moonlit thoughts whisper, drawing near.
Gentle breezes caress our skin,
In this quietude, we feel the kin.

Reflections dance on the tranquil lake,
Each ripple carries the dreams we make.
Stars twinkle softly, guiding our way,
In the stillness of night, we choose to stay.

A tapestry woven with laughter and sighs,
Tender moments, no need for disguise.
Together we cherish this peaceful glow,
In moonlit realms, our spirits flow.

Silence wrapped in the warmth of grace,
In the heart's refuge, we find our space.
Serenity beckons, a festive vibe,
In moonlit thoughts, forever we thrive.

Hibernating Hearts in the Whispering Woods

In the woods where the whispers reside,
Hibernating hearts seek warmth inside.
Each leaf a blanket, soft and kind,
Time slows down, allowing peace to unwind.

The crackle of branches beneath our feet,
Nature's lullaby, a rhythmic beat.
Joy is the spark in the frostbit air,
In these quiet woods, we find our care.

Snowflakes fall like dreams from above,
Each flurry a token of winter's love.
Together we feast on the magic around,
In hibernating hearts, joy is profound.

Embracing the whispers, the chill we defy,
With laughter and stories, our spirits fly.
In the woods we celebrate, warm and bright,
Hibernating hearts glowing in the night.

When Night Holds Its Breath

When stars twinkle bright in the dark,
Laughter dances, igniting a spark.
The air is sweet, filled with delight,
As joy blooms beneath the soft moonlight.

Winter whispers secrets so dear,
Echoes of friendship draw us near.
With every cheer, we gather close,
In this moment, we feel morose.

Candles flicker, casting warm glows,
Around us, the spirit of love grows.
A feast awaits, laughter will flow,
Tonight we share, the warmth of the show.

As night holds its breath, we unite,
Embracing the magic, holding tight.
With hearts aglow and spirits high,
We cherish these moments, you and I.

Nested in Winter's Embrace

In nests of snow, where silence gleams,
We find the warmth of our childhood dreams.
With hot cocoa, we gather inside,
Wrapped in love, a cozy tide.

Frosted windows bloom with light,
As laughter carries through the night.
Gaily we share stories untold,
Magic woven in threads of gold.

Outside, snowflakes twirl in delight,
As nature dons her gown so white.
With each breath, the world feels new,
In this embrace, we feel the true.

Nested in warmth against the cold,
Our hearts are open, stories unfold.
In winter's hug, we feel our place,
Together we find joy in this space.

Reflections Beneath the Frost

Beneath the frost, the world glimmers bright,
We wander through this enchanting night.
With every step, the crunching sound,
Whispers of joy freshly abound.

Ornaments sparkle on every tree,
Telling tales of love and glee.
The air is filled with a merry tune,
As hearts embrace the coming moon.

In the glow of fireside grace,
We share our hopes in warm embrace.
Reflections dance in each other's eyes,
A tapestry spun beneath the skies.

Beneath the frost, the magic's alive,
In every laugh, we thrive and strive.
Holding hands, facing the chill,
With friendships strong, we find our thrill.

Echoes of the Quiet Midwinter

In stillness deep, where echoes play,
Midwinter holds its peaceful sway.
Softly we gather, voices align,
Companions in this sweet divine.

Fires flicker, casting golden light,
Creating warmth on this joyous night.
With stories shared and spirits free,
In every moment, we find glee.

The world outside may feel so cold,
But here inside, our hearts are bold.
We toast to life, to love, to cheer,
Echoes of laughter fill the year.

As midwinter speaks in whispers soft,
We cherish memories, memories loft.
Together we stand, united strong,
In this festive time, where we belong.

Reverie of the Sun's Retreat

Golden rays bid the day goodbye,
Shadows dance in the evening sky.
Laughter rings through the air so sweet,
As hearts gather in a joyous beat.

Candles flicker, the night begins,
With whispered tales and gentle grins.
The world slows down in twilight's embrace,
Love and warmth in every face.

Stars awaken, they twinkle bright,
Lighting dreams with their silver light.
Underneath this canopy wide,
Hope and wonder swell inside.

Celebrate the magic found,
In the fleeting moments, joy abound.
Together we share this vibrant scene,
In the reverie, we weave our dream.

Twilight's Gentle Lullaby

The sun dips low, a soft caress,
Nature sighs in peacefulness.
Whispers float on the evening breeze,
As laughter mingles amidst the trees.

Fireflies blink in a playful game,
Chasing shadows, never the same.
A serenade of colors blend,
In this twilight, worries mend.

Glistening stars peek from above,
Wrapping the world in a cloak of love.
Hearts unite in this tranquil hour,
As dreams awaken, so sweetly flower.

In gentle rhythms, the night unfolds,
A tapestry of stories told.
With each heartbeat, joy does sigh,
In the embrace of twilight's lullaby.

When Stars Take Their Time

Night drapes softly, a velvet sheet,
As time slows down, the world's heartbeat.
Stars twinkle slowly, each a bright gem,
We gather close, lost in the whim.

The hush of night, a calming grace,
A gentle smile on each glowing face.
Cider warms in our waiting hands,
As laughter ripples through the lands.

Moonlight dances on shimmering ponds,
In this place where magic responds.
Every glance holds a hidden tale,
In this moment where dreams set sail.

With wishes whispered and secrets shared,
A tapestry of love, gently paired.
In every sparkle, in every rhyme,
We cherish the night when stars take their time.

Crystalline Dreams at Dusk

Dusk descends, a shimmering veil,
Painting the sky in a vibrant trail.
Crystalline dreams begin to rise,
Bathed in the glow of twilight skies.

With notes of laughter, stories blend,
In these moments, joy transcends.
Softly we gather, hand in hand,
As the world transforms, beautifully planned.

The stars awaken, one by one,
Ushering in the night's fun.
Each flicker a promise, each glow a cheer,
Whispering secrets for all to hear.

In this dance of light, we sway,
Embracing each magic-filled day.
Crystalline dreams, our hearts ignite,
In a festive glow of pure delight.

Chaos of the Year Grounded in Stillness

Colors twirl in the bustling parade,
Laughter rings out, a joyous cascade.
Fireworks spark in the shadowed skies,
While dreams dance wild in the festival's eyes.

Whispers of joy on the breezy night,
Glimmers of hope in the soft candlelight.
Voices entwined in a melodious cheer,
Each heart beats vibrant, a rhythm sincere.

In the whirlwind of moments, we find our place,
Unity shines in this boisterous space.
Though chaos surrounds with its festive cheer,
We pause in the stillness, our spirits clear.

With friends gathered 'round, we raise a glass,
To memories made, like the seasons, they pass.
The chaos will fade, but love remains bright,
Grounded in stillness, we bask in the light.

Respite of the Frigid Dawn

Softly the light breaks the winter's embrace,
Frosted leaves shimmer, a delicate lace.
The world holds its breath in the quiet of morn,
Awakening dreams on the cusp of the dawn.

Candles flicker in the chill of the air,
Gathering warmth in this moment we share.
Laughter spills forth, a cascade of joy,
At the table set for every girl and boy.

With cocoa in hand and hearts open wide,
We revel together, no reason to hide.
The frigid dawn carries whispers of cheer,
In this festive respite, we hold each other near.

As light dances softly on snow-laden trees,
We celebrate warmth in the crisp, biting breeze.
The dawn may be frigid, but spirits are bright,
In our hearts, a glow that overcomes night.

Veils of Frost under a Silent Moon

Beneath the silent moon, the world is aglow,
Veils of frost shimmer, a magical show.
Stars twinkle bright in the velvet expanse,
While dreams swirl like snowflakes in whimsical dance.

Gather close, loved ones, the night whispers sweet,
As laughter entwines in the softest heartbeat.
With stories of old and hopes for the new,
We cradle the joy that is wrapped in the blue.

In this wonderland kissed by the frost,
We cherish the moments, no time to be lost.
The moonlight is festive, a guide through the dark,
Igniting our spirits, rekindling the spark.

So let us unite in this sparkling night,
With hearts drawn together, our spirits take flight.
Under the veils of frost, love reigns supreme,
In the silent moonlight, we revel and dream.

The Beauty in Waning Light

As daylight retreats, the horizon ignites,
A canvas of colors, a dance of delights.
The sun dips low, painting skies with its gold,
While shadows grow long, the evening unfolds.

Gathered together, with warmth in our hearts,
We savor each moment as the dusk gently starts.
With laughter like music, we share in the glow,
Of candles that flicker, a soft amber flow.

The beauty in waning light captures our souls,
Transforming the mundane, making each moment whole.
In unity wrapped, we welcome the night,
With hope interwoven in every soft light.

So let celebration rise with the stars overhead,
As stories are shared and sweet memories spread.
In the beauty of twilight, our spirits take flight,
Together forever in love's joyous light.

www.ingramcontent.com/pod-product-compliance
Ingram Content Group UK Ltd.
Pitfield, Milton Keynes, MK11 3LW, UK
UKHW030853221224
452712UK00006B/260